581
MIN

MINER, O. IRENE SEVREY

PLANTS WE KNOW

	DATE DUE		
2-5			
2BL			

A New True Book

PLANTS WE KNOW

By O. Irene Sevrey Miner

This "true book" was prepared
under the direction of
Illa Podendorf,
formerly with the Laboratory School,
University of Chicago

CHILDRENS PRESS, CHICAGO

PHOTO CREDITS

Lynn M. Stone—4 (top), 7, 19, 22 (lower right), 29 (top), 31, 33, 39 (above right), 42 (bottom)

James P. Rowan—Cover, 6, 8, 9, 24, 40, 41

Art Thoma—10, 34 (middle)

Candee & Associates—4 (bottom), 29 (middle)

Margrit Fiddle—2, 28 (2 photos), 30 (top)

Texas State Department of Highways & Public Transportation: 26, 34 (bottom)

Tony Freeman—13, 37, 42

Jerry Hennen—21, 22 (top), 44

Margaret Thoma—17, 22 (lower left), 45

United States Department of Agriculture: USDA—34, 36, 38, 39 (top)

The Rice Council—39 (left)

Len Meents—14, 16, 18, 20

Library of Congress Cataloging in Publication Data

Miner, O. Irene Sevrey (Opal Irene Sevrey), 1906-
  Plants we know.

  (A New true book)
  Previously published as: The true book of plants we know. 1953.
  Summary: Briefly introduces different kinds of plants, their parts, how they grow, and their benefits to man.
  1. Plants—Juvenile literature. [1. Plants]
I. Title.
QK49.M6 1981   581   81-9929
ISBN 0-516-01642-3   AACR2

  10 11 12 13 14 15 16 17 18 19 20 R 99 98 97 96 95 94

TABLE OF CONTENTS

Flower garden

Cornfield

PLANTS WE KNOW

We know many kinds of plants.

Some grow on land.

Plants grow...

    in our houses,

    in fields,

    in yards,

    in greenhouses, and

    in forests.

Water lily

Some grow in water...
in lakes or
in ponds.

Edge of the
timberline
in Olympic
Mountains

Many grow in high places.

Many grow in low places.

Mangroves in Everglades National Park

Some grow in swamps.

Some grow in deserts.

Yucca in Monument Valley

PLANTS LARGE AND SMALL

All plants grow.

Some plants grow big and tall. Trees grow tall.

Some trees grow taller than other trees. They may grow a great deal taller than our houses.

Shrubs grow tall, but not as tall as trees.

Some plants stay small. Garden plants stay small. Most house plants are small. Most grasses are little plants.

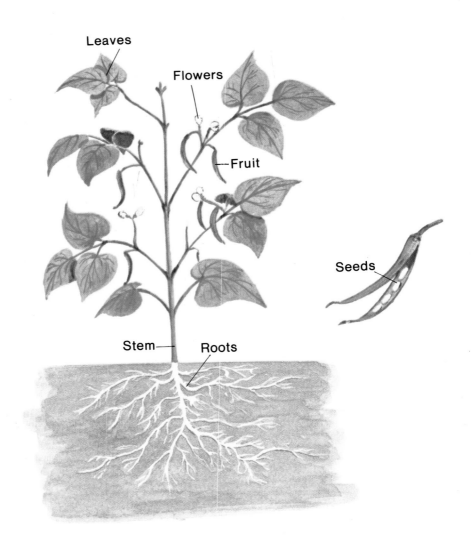

Leaves

Flowers

Fruit

Seeds

Stem

Roots

PARTS OF PLANTS

Many plants have parts
which we know.

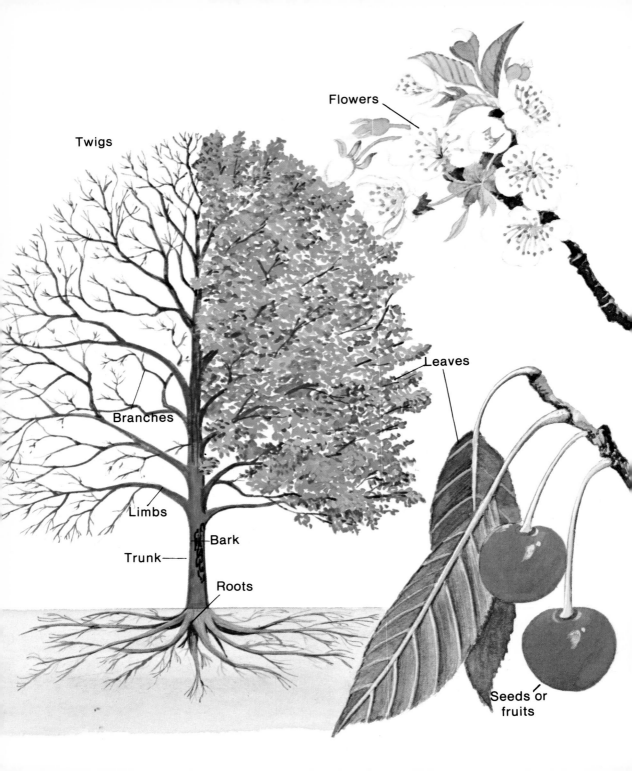

Twigs

Flowers

Branches

Leaves

Limbs

Bark

Trunk

Roots

Seeds or fruits

Some trees have these same parts and some other parts, too.

Did you see that tree stems are called trunks? Tree stems or trunks are woody.

Some trees have no
flowers or leaves. Here are
their parts.

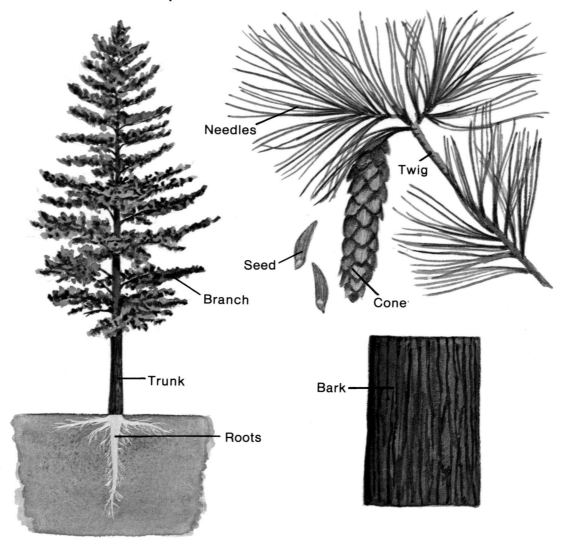

Needles

Twig

Seed

Branch

Cone

Trunk

Bark

Roots

Ponderosa pine cones

Did you see what these
trees have in place of
flowers and leaves?

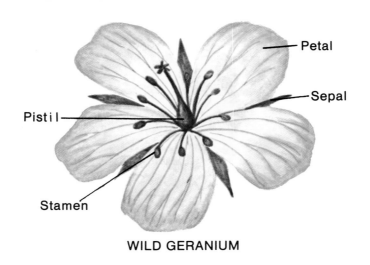

Petal

Sepal

Pistil

Stamen

WILD GERANIUM

PARTS OF FLOWERS

Some flowers have pretty colors.

These flowers have special parts.

Not all flowers are easy to see. But all flowers have stamens or pistils.

Crab apple in bloom

Fruit may grow from flowers.

Seeds may grow inside the fruit.

Seeds may grow inside cones, too.

Aspen trees

Virginia creeper (ivy)

Shrub in winter

WAYS PLANTS GROW

Trees are plants with one trunk.

Shrubs are plants with many trunks.

Vines are plants that climb.

Fern

Many plants do not have woody stems like trees. Their stems are green.

Plants may grow in bunches.

They may grow alone.

WAYS PLANTS GROW NEW PLANTS

Many kinds of plants
come from seeds.

Grass comes from
seeds.

Many flowers come from
seeds.

Orange tree with blossoms

Many fruits come from seeds.

Many vegetables come from seeds.

Some seeds are larger than others.

Some seeds are smaller than others.

Philodendron

Geraniums

Some plants do not grow
from seeds.
Some grow from stems
or pieces of stem.

Daffodil

Tulips

Some grow from roots.
Some grow from bulbs.

African
violets

Some grow from leaves
of a mother plant.
Some grow from buds
which are on an
underground stem.

Potato
harvest

Maple leaves

WHAT PLANTS NEED TO GROW

The green parts of plants make food. The green parts are the leaves and sometimes the stems.

Leaves need water to make food. Rain gives the plants water. Wilted plants need water.

Leaves need air to make food. They use the carbon dioxide in the air.

The sun helps the plants
grow. The sun gives the
plants heat and light. The
plants are yellow if they
do not have light.

Soybeans

Cabbage field

HOW PLANTS STORE FOOD

Some plants store food
on top of the ground...
in seeds,
in stems,
in fruits, or
in leaves.
Some plants store food
underground...
in roots, or
in underground stems.

Harvesting
lettuce

PARTS OF PLANTS
WE EAT

We eat parts of plants.
We eat the leaves of
cabbage and lettuce.
We eat stalks of celery
and rhubarb.

We eat buds and stems of asparagus.

We eat flowers of cauliflower.

We eat bulbs of onions.

We eat roots of radishes, beets, and carrots.

Harvesting apples

We eat fruits of plants such as apples, peaches, tomatoes, and raspberries. We eat seeds such as peas, beans, rice, and wheat. Nuts are seeds, too.

Top: Peaches
Above right: Tomatoes
Left: Rice

HOW WE NEED PLANTS

Plants give us other things besides food. Can you think of other ways we use plants?

Did you think of cotton clothing?

Cotton field

Gerbil

Did you think of food for your pet?

Look at the next page. You will find more uses of plants there.

Plants give us food.

Hay field

We need plants for our food.

We need plants to feed our farm animals.

We need plants to give us food to feed our pets.

We need parts of plants to make cloth or clothing.

We need plants for building.

Young raccoon in a tree hollow

Daisies

We need plants for homes for animals.

We need plants for making furniture.

We need plants to make our world prettier.

WORDS YOU SHOULD KNOW

asparagus (uh • SPAR • uh • gus)—a plant whose stalk is eaten as a vegetable

bark—the outer covering of the trunks, branches, and roots of trees

blossom (BLOS • um)—a flower

branch—part of the tree or shrub that grows out from the trunk or limb

bulb—a plant part which is round and if put into soil, a new plant grows from it

celery (SELL • uh • ree)—a plant which is eaten as a vegetable

climb (KLYM)—to grow upward by holding on to something

Earth (ERTH)—the planet on which we live

float (FLOTE)—to move on the top of the water

fruit (FROOT)—the part of a plant that has the seeds

garden plants—plants that grow outdoors

grass—a green plant with narrow leaves

house plants—plants that grow indoors

leaf—the thin, flat, green part of a plant that grows from the stem

limb (LIM)—a large branch of a tree or shrub

lumber (LUM • ber)—wood from a tree or shrub

orchard (OR • cherd)—land where fruit trees grow

petal (PET • ul)—one of a flower's often brightly colored leaves

pistil (PIST • ul)—a flower part that produces the seed

rhubarb (ROO • barb)—a plant whose stalk is eaten as food

ride—to be carried along

root—the part of a plant that usually grows down into the ground

sail(SAYL)—to move easily

seed—the part of a flowering plant that can grow into a new plant

sepal (SEE•pul)—usually a green, leaf-like part of a plant found on the outside of a flower

shrub—a woody plant that is smaller than a tree and has several separate stems rather than a single trunk

slip—a part of a plant cut or broken off and used to grow a new plant

stalk—main stem of a plant

stamen (STAY•mun)—a plant part at the center of a flower that holds pollen-bearing parts

stem—main supporting part of a plant; stalk

trunk—tall main stem of a tree

twig—small branch of a tree or shrub

vine—a plant with a climbing stem

INDEX

About the Author

Irene Miner, an educator, developed this book in answer to the need for informative material for the beginning reader. In addition to her writing for children, the author enjoys painting, ceramics, photography, carpentry, and collecting stones and rocks.